American Light

American Light

POEMS BY
MICHAEL PETTIT

The University of Georgia Press

Athens

Copyright © 1984 by Michael Pettit
Published by the University of Georgia Press
Athens, Georgia 30602

All rights reserved
Set in 10 on 12 point Palatino
Printed in the United States of America

Library of Congress Cataloging in Publication Data

Pettit, Michael.
  American light.

  I. Title.
PS3566.E89A8 1983   811'.54   83-5773
ISBN 0-8203-0675-4
ISBN 0-8203-0677-0 (pbk.)

for Annie Mae and Guy Cowden
and for Gene Ann and Ed

Acknowledgments

Some of the poems in this book have appeared previously. Grateful acknowledgment is due the editors of the following publications:

Beloit Poetry Journal: "The Life of the Mind in a Field of Hay" under the title "Coastal Bermuda Hay,""Peace and Quiet" under the title "Peace and Quiet Are Not the Same Thing"

Black Warrior Review: "Cape Work," "Celestial," "Fire and Ice," "Self-Portrait Approaching Promontory, Utah"

Intro 12 (Associated Writing Programs): "Sundays, Our Summer of Perpetual Rain," "To Let Go"

The Missouri Review: "Cardinal," "Looney Tunes," "Without Fear"

The New Virginia Review: "Herdsman" (section 1), "Those Who Stay On"

Sand: "Fence Work" under the title "The Poet Builds Fence"

Texas Stories and Poems: "Open Water"

I wish to thank the University of Alabama for a fellowship which enabled me to complete this book.

M.P.

Contents

III

I

Looney Tunes

About suffering they were never wrong . . .
W. H. AUDEN

1

The bright primary colors
of the test pattern play
on his face, cupped in his hands,
a white rose offered up
to the light. Outside
the sun is no more awake
than he is, yawning, sleep
still in his eyes as he sits
watching, cross-legged, three feet
from the screen. But watch him
come alive, fidget and twitch,
his soft feet wriggling
in the flannel feet of his PJ's,
sugar from his Trix speeding
through his veins, high-pitched
whine of the TV singing
to his nerves. He can't wait,
can't stand what is static—
all that lacks animation,
does not breathe, move, struggle,
all in which the fury of life
is too slow to be seen.

2

Ah Bugs, wise-ass rabbit,
he watches you, thrilled by your style,
the way you escape disaster
and leisurely chew a carrot

as you deliver the wicked and just
reward. Such wit in one with a furry
tail and long ears, walking upright!
And he listens to the smart-mouth duck,
the stuttering pig, squabbling
dogs and cats, mouse in the walls,
bird in his cage, roadrunner running
the coyote ragged across the desert.
Animals, Bugs, animals
and the fall of man. You slip
the dynamite back to the little man
with red mustaches, blow him sky high
and he falls. The famished coyote,
too sly for his own good, is always
falling: he rockets or runs off a cliff
into thin air. When the slender
branch that saves him tears loose
at the roots, it's the long fall,
the whistling fall toward the canyon
floor. Impact sends up a doughnut
of dust we watch from above.
And of course like the coyote
he wanders away from the screen—
hungry, Bugs, and in for it.

3

Animus, spirit, hostility—
in his little heart he loves
best what is most explosive,
loud yellow flashes that lift him
into hysterics. He tumbles
around on the floor with his pillow,
cheering Daffy and Porky forever after
one another's hide. They whale away

with whatever Providence supplies:
ancient bow and arrow, catapult
and boulder, shotgun, firepower
of the radio-controlled rocket.
There's a bull's-eye on everything,
everyone, on the coyote's nose
when the beep-beep over the rise
is a Greyhound bus. That's *life*
and he loves it! Technicolor
sparks, pain all Saturday morning,
bringing out the beast in him.
Tasmanian devil with milk on his lip,
his heart goes out, hot and urgent,
to the one in pursuit—damn
the anvils dropping from the sky,
damn the train in the tunnel,
the tunnel painted on solid rock—
onward, upward, into bits and pieces.

4

And what's nice is
how little it matters how gone
you are. Take him—no prince of bop
tooting cocaine was ever quite
this gone—lost and loving
the red and green and blue
world of simple cells, starfish world
of regeneration. At her spinning wheel
fuddlebrained Granny will unravel
Sylvester's fur and he'll whirl,
a top disappearing turn by turn.
But bless her, her feeble hands
and her knitting needles, she'll
bring him back again, wide-eyed

on the back of a sweater. Catch that
flow. And see what happens when
lightning strikes Porky, who's reduced
to bones glowing behind a raincoat—
nothing, nothing lasting. He knows
it's nine lives for all the animals,
ten cartoons an hour, every single
Saturday morning. When Porky sputters
"Th-th-that's all folks" it's not,
not by a long shot. The gun going off
in your face leaves it black
but still intact and the whole show,
miraculous and everlasting, goes on.

5

Compliment your maker, Bugs,
on leaving off the fifth finger.
It doesn't take long, this movement
toward real flesh, before it pales,
comes up short of what he wants.
The wet smack on the lips you give
Elmer is sweet enough, but then
Popeye enters, scrapping with Brutus
over the disgusting Olive Oyl.
All too human—like his parents,
still in bed, angelic, his father's hand
asleep between his mother's legs.
At least in a pinch Popeye's fists
turn to battleships, guns blazing.
When the Sugar Crisp Bear gives way
to Sun-Lovin' Malibu Barbie, complete
with strap marks—well Bugs, it's gone
too far. Even Roy Rogers can't get by
without Dale, Trigger without Buttermilk.

You're a *rabbit* and you don't seem to
need that stuff, that mush, that goo.
At noon real life—old movies, baseball—
takes over, and who needs it? Not him.
Pillow in hand he goes off to play out
the afternoon in his room with some moose
or panda or hippo. Behind his door
it's the Congo—drums, bird cries,
witch doctors with painted faces. Go
to him Bugs. He's impatient, waiting
with wide eyes among the red and white
flowers that can eat you alive.

Mr. Ho's

Either it doesn't help
or it isn't needed.
FORTUNE COOKIE

Cheers from Mr. Ho, who can't stand
simplicity, who each year adds
more gaudy New Year's bunting, more
tinsel and froufrou to his ceiling
and walls and tables. I take a seat
and he's on me, hustling his Fogcutters,
his Navy Grog, offering me everything
in the bartender's fat book.
I have a No thank you for each,
a No please for all the appetizers,
a No for the veil Ho's Chinese bellydancer
flounces across my neck as I wait for
my sweet and sour pork. Can't they see
I am here for simple Chinese fare
and not to cure some melancholy?
Perhaps the drunk across the room
needed his last flaming drink
and it may have helped to tuck
his dollar next to the bellydancer's
creamy skin, to hear her ululations
and watch her ass shimmy away
in her gauzy pantaloons. It seems so:
now he's smiling and Ho is smiling
and she is smiling, looming over me
with her perfume and sweat, hot
for a tip. But it is my neck,
my night to hang my head and goddamn
if I want this, want anything
but my pork, stale cookie and the check.

Fire and Ice

From my couch I rise, afire
with Zeno and cosmic conflagration,
to answer. Through the screen door
the mild faces of two Latter Day Saints
smile up at me like seal cubs
from an ice floe. Their shirts
are white, their blue suits creased,
their ponderous shoes tied.
Door to door go their days, face
to frowning face, but I
will not share their message.
Behind me the room floats
with the smoke of cigarettes,
one for each question I have.
Can they answer whether God
is the fiery mind of the world?
Whether chaos or order reigns,
whether it is collapse forever
or just for now? The one who is
the scrubbed blonde they all are
is speaking as I close the door.
His voice weakens like the cries
of a seal puzzled by his blood
splashed across the ice. Go, go.
Your time is up. *Thou art a little*
soul bearing about a corpse.

Self-Portrait Approaching
Promontory, Utah

Again today it is
disciplined thought I'm after,
clear as the blue mountain
air into which a white boa of smoke
rises. Below, naturally,
is the locomotive and I think
about trains of thought, how long
they are, coal car after coal car
after coal car pulling up the grade.
Think about the rails and ties,
about the rock roadbed
and the grease on the rocks
and the stubs of flares
and the conductor in the caboose
with its pot-bellied stove,
and the pot-bellied engineer
with his head out the window,
spitting tobacco, his hand resting
on the wide-open throttle.
And think what would happen
if slowly and for no reason
he knows, the conductor starts
to uncouple the cars, caboose first,
then coal car after coal car
after coal car. The leaping conductor
bidding each in turn good-bye,
unattached and in perfect order
they'd go rolling back down
the mountain so that the smoke
from the smokestack blows
horizontal as the scenery

slowly goes by faster and faster
until the engineer finally notices
and spits and thinks Shit
now what could be happening now?

Cape Work

Comes my mercurial woman, kazoo
of a heart buzzing and her breasts
pink with it. You'd think it
wasn't anger that so moves her
down the street, but love. The way
her legs are in motion but her eye
is fixed is lovely. She sees
the cape I'm waving, red satin,
and would do me in except for
the flourish—once around the body
and I'm naked, no suit of lights.
Later, my ear against her belly,
it's not Sousa I hear and not
a thousand banjoes. Not brass,
strings, woodwinds, drums beneath
her skin. It's a white noise,
and heartless, as if my head lay
on a pillow of down and she
were gone or going or never there.

Pop Fly to Short Center

The fat pitch loops
in over the plate.
At the moment of contact,
the moment of maximum
compression, the ball is
as motionless as
the universe allows.
Breathless from last play
the centerfielder
is telling himself he will
stop smoking. The shortstop
pictures his last error.
The secondbaseman thinks
0 for 4. The ball rises
in another world. Rises,
stops, drops toward a point
on the earth to which
three figures are rushing,
arms outstretched.
When they touch all life
will begin again: the fat
pitch lobbed in over
the plate and the batter
swinging wildly, in a world
he shares with other immortals.

Without Fear

All the dogs sleeping
on the dark front lawns awake
at once and are up, barking
into the warm night air.
July: the light of the street lamp
on the street is a cool moon.
Into it move a boy and girl
in no hurry, each step
a loss they are sure to feel.
But only much later: white,
his softball uniform shines
and the dogs bark louder.
She holds his hand, without fear
if he is, and he is. Sounds
of the softball field no longer
reach him, but no matter,
here too he is without fear.
To the dogs he bows, deeply,
toward their furious forms
in the dark yards. He bows,
but it is not enough: he sits
down in the center of the street.
She holds on, bending to him,
her hair dropping from her shoulders
as he sweeps off his cap
to the dogs, the night, everything.
The barking stops for a moment
when life is almost perfect:
if only she would fall into his arms
there under the street lamp.
The dogs start. Lights come on
in the houses. And he rises,

undefeated, puts on his cap.
They go off down the block
toward the traffic light, the still
intersection changing color
to color. It takes them forever
to walk out of sight, and longer
before the dogs fall silent.

Sundays, Our Summer of Perpetual Rain

Under umbrellas the congregation
stands on the church steps,
shaking hands. The sermon
on good works, the week in review.
One voice with the rain, their song
is steady. No flights
of high notes cross the road
to wake us, no refrain
rolls us back to sleep.

Our sleep is steady. Oak and fir
and hickory catch the rain,
drop it from needles and leaves.
The earth is soft, moss
higher on the trunks each week.
Summer will not take hold.
The nights are cool and daylight
never makes it through the trees.
Our walls of stone grow green
and slick, the windows fog,
doors swell shut, the steps
are treacherous. All summer

we sleep in. Nothing but light
could drive us from our bed.
We hear the engines catch
and idle before they die off
down the wet roads. As the minister
caresses one last hand in his,
we take hold of each other.

Cardinal

Outside, the days come, alike
with their sunlight and summer heat,
extended like a hand
in which you see no weapon.
It is there: the day comes
and he comes, crimson flash
from the surrounding green.
Senseless beautiful bird,
he sends himself through the air
to crash against a window
then flutter back, stunned,
to the trees. Among the needles
of the pine, in the funerary willows,
in the bamboo grown straight
and tall around an inner emptiness,
he rests, recovers to come again.
A state of siege: what first seemed
accident takes on purpose.
Cardinal, songbird that does not sing,
he comes to shatter the quiet
you keep inside for him to shatter.
At any moment his body will rattle
a window, the room, the whole house
and you cannot deny you want
nothing else. Impossible to say
where he'll strike next: you
count twenty windows and not one
is without its small star of blood.
You go from one to another, looking
into the trees, offering yourself
to the sunlight and to his eye, cocked
and watching. You hope he will

spread his red wings and his heart
will race and he will fly toward
the window where you wait,
behind a feathery spot of fire
in the clear glass, growing larger,
matching him wingbeat for wingbeat
as he comes on. As he comes on
you'll see what is mirrored
in his eyes, the joy that drives him.
And something else, a terror
he must subdue, take inside,
filling his senseless beautiful body.

American Light

What glory when the Luminists
return from the sea
at sunset. Against the horizon
they file by, long white coats
brushing sea oats and grasses
along the sandy paths,
stirring fireflies into flight
behind them. Each in his arms
carries canvases where the skies
shape everything: even the ocean
is the work of light. Light
surges from the clouds to color
the shore—sand, waves breaking
on the reef, a shipwreck
collapsing into shadows. How cold
and clear their colors are.
At dusk the Luminists walk
toward home and chromatic dreams
of their ancestors—the glowworm,
lightning, the aurora borealis—
in full display. Let the French
rise from the water lily,
American light is no less.
Luminescent, it will flourish.

They were not wrong. Everywhere
you see their descendents—
red neon signs of bars and motels,
televisions emptying blue snow
into silent bedrooms.
Other nights you wake to stare
at the yellow-green faces

of alarm clocks, radar screens,
x-rays of your bones. Their light
is the light you live by,
the Luminists in their graves
are satisfied: cool to touch
and to the eye, fluorescent
lamps glow in museums above
their canvases, the sky above all,
all with their glossy finish.

Open Water

Recidivist, standing where you stand
each night to watch each night deepen,

you have memory—scars on the brain,
fractures in the ice on a pond,

deep or shallow. You remember the alphabet,
your times tables, one recurrent

childhood dream. A birthday cake floats
in a dark that is bottomless, limitless,

terrifying. There's a white ribbon
you must walk across toward the cake,

its one candle yours to wish upon
and blow out. Then your dreams, real enough,

begin. You listen to their faint sound,
remember the future you saw for yourself

one cold night. Standing still and quiet
as the movement of winter over buildings

where others study, their pages and windows lit,
you hear the eerie, icy calling.

Then quick a ripple across the moon,
the vee of the Canada geese, trapped

in a midnight flight, crying so.
Calling for open water to shine like light

in the dark below, they cross your life,
a thousand lives from Manitoba to Louisiana.

II

Do not believe that we can live
today in the country
for the country will bring us
no peace.
WILLIAM CARLOS WILLIAMS

Herdsman

1

Here I am whole, I know
at night what I'll find come
morning: skies violet in the west,
a crown of light to the east.
I'll wake, a rainbow:
I don't come out until the storm
is over. Dreams I leave behind.

Here I've learned the cycles last
and how to live within them,
with the brindle dog at my doorstep,
gnawing a bone dragged in from
the woods, dug from the green
circle of earth where I burn
and bury the cattle that winter kills.

And with this: huge red bulls
following their own breath
over the frosted pastures. Gaunt,
sleepless, rutting through the herd
as calves butt their mothers' bags
for more of the blue-white milk.
Here one gold day follows another.

2

It is Euell Hitt's errant Brangus
cow again and there is one answer.
I unleash my curs at the edge

of the swamp thicket where she hides—
loco, motionless among black leaves
and shadows, waiting. It won't take
long: her scent is fresh, the story
old as those endless prairies of snow
where Arctic winds swirl around
the exhausted caribou, the circling
timber wolves. Winter by winter,
common cells dividing, moving slow
as ice, they've arrived. I hear
snarl and bellow and the brush
gives way: Euell's cow backs out
into the open. Hornless, head lowered,
she stumbles with rage, feigning charges
that the dogs take lightly, grinning,
driving her in flurries toward
the pens, the short ride home.
Black as the deepest wood, in the pens
she stands shivering, bright blood
on her lips, tongue hanging tipped
with blood. With one look she tells me
it is not over, it will never be.

3

I dream of the night
I'll do it, undress and walk out
into the fields, unearthly,
lit by the crescent moon.
Where there was a hillside,
cows and their calves bedded down,
a herd of steady breathing, breathing,
the wind will travel the hill
to me alone. The grass will move,
thick and tall and untouched

until I lie down, and sleep.
It is in sleep she comes to me,
curious, hesitant, ready
to break at my first motion.
With her rough black tongue
she licks the back of my neck,
my cheek, my eyes. I know, I know—
she has been everywhere, looking
for me. There is no hope unless
I give in and never go back.

Peace and Quiet

At the exact moment the queen of Carnival
is crowned in New Orleans, ninety miles

away, farmboys from the dry counties
of south Mississippi plow down Bourbon Street,

breaking a crust of bottles and beer cans,
their eyes gleaming like disc blades.

At the exact moment the whole show goes
wild and from balconies streamers of purple,

gold and green winnow down through the uproar,
I'm at work here, stabbing a posthole

into the hard clay earth off Valley Road,
sweating out the beer I drank before leaving.

A pickup passes, raising dust and dust
fills the air as I rest, hot, out of breath.

I've hit rock a foot down, not deep enough
to stop and the gatepost must go here:

I didn't leave to dig around stone. I left
to strike this one spot in this dry county,

to spend muscle and will against buried rock,
to hear my breath lunge, burning in my throat,

and I came to rest for this one moment, rest
and listen to the still air as the earth

draws the dust down, as quiet gathers,
tightens, a heart forcing one last beat.

Postmortem

Homer Moody does not shit around.
I watch him pull off the highway
and race across the rough pasture.
A busy man, there's no waste
in his life: jaw set, he's come to work
and works fast. I watch him split
the calf I found stiff this morning.
With his short, curved blade he slices
hide, muscle, cartilage, bone.
Cattle herd around us, watching,
a still black corona that flares away
when he snaps the rib cage open.
How easy it seems. His hands
go into the bright arrangement
of lungs, stomach, intestines, heart.
Each he examines and moves aside.
On the highway, a passing truck blares
its horn. It's dead too long,
he tells me, to say for sure:
possible pneumonia. His voice, low
and level, seems to soothe the cattle
reassembling closer than ever,
silent, a score of curious faces.
At the point of his knife I see
the lesions, small dark purple blooms
on the lungs. It's all he can offer,
a bouquet of death I can accept
or not. As the calf goes back together
in proper order, he tells me he'll send
a sample to the lab in Starkville
if I find the next one quicker.
Scrubbing blood from his elbows down,

snapping his knife shut, Homer
takes a last slow look at the circle
of cattle, not speaking but willing
to answer a final question,
if I ask and if there is an answer.

Fence Work

1

Wire sagging where staples have worked free
of the posts, posts rotted at ground level

by years of insects and bad weather, standing
out of habit between two fields, ragged

suggestion in the wandering minds of cattle,
the old fence must come down. It resists,

with rusted barbs sharp as ever, tangles
of wild rose and blackberry vines, a trellis

of thorns where guinea wasps and yellow jackets
hang out of sight on nests as big as my hand.

Bush-knife, hammer and nail-pull, a half-mile
of sweat, working one old post then the next,

each grown roots like a dead man his beard,
staples buried beneath ridges of scar tissue

I burst with hammer-blows until, with a jerk,
the last wire sails free—trailing twenty years'

growth of wild rose and brambles and weeds.
When I snap the posts off, it is done.

2

Steel of a claw hammer,
of staples and twentypenny nails,

of wire stretcher, quarter-mile
coils of new barbed wire,
shovel blades of steel,
the steel post maul

the wood of each handle,
of hammer, shovel, pick,
wood of a hundred new posts
heavy and black with creosote,
line, brace and corner posts
to anchor the steel

to a bare field, sun-shot,
no shadow for a half-mile
in any direction, a field
of short grass, bitterweed,
carelessweed, fire-ant beds
red as the sun overhead

3

Wood. Steel. Sun.
The last hammer-blow rings
a half-mile down the line.

In the evening light I walk
the fence for the first time
to see if the wire is tight:

it snaps back and sings.
Somewhere in the grass
a bobwhite answers, in key.

I strike the second wire

and killdeer rise behind me,
crying and circling back.

A flight of mourning doves
homes on the third string,
blackbirds caw to the fourth.

In succession I snap
the wires: I hear quail,
killdeer, dove and redwing.

Light flaring at sunset,
my heart and arm swinging,
I dance along the new fence,

hammer striking wire
and wood and the field
where the field birds sing.

Jewel Wheat

Not just Jewel. He was his mama's
Precious Jewel. He gives me the smile
she got fifty years ago: shy, tongue
pink where his teeth are gone.
Laughter jiggles the round belly
he picked up in a Bogalusa roadhouse,
same place he lost his teeth. Fighting
over some woman, drunk. Mornings
he didn't show for work it was sick.
Jewel called it the flu and it struck
when his wallet came full, lasted
a week until his money ran out.
Groceries, rent, child support, bills
for his medicine: money went quick.
So he'd work, slow as summer, sweaty,
puffing, his round face the tint
of rosé wine. Each break I got the story
of his life. How after the war
he hauled pulpwood for Crown Zellerbach,
sunup to sundown for five years
until a sweetgum shattered his leg.
How it took him a whole seven months
at the Biloxi V.A. with nothing to do
but lie there and heal and watch the Gulf
out his window. After that he couldn't
take on more than changing tires
or tractor work. Nothing too heavy.
He liked it fine if they treated you
right. He'd driven for Virgil Burge,
Hollis Thigpen, Dawsie Barber, but I
understood a man can only do so much.
Precious Jewel. How blue and tiny his eyes

were in his pink face. How he'd sing
above the sound of his tractor, riding
along raking those windrows he never could
make follow the contours of the field.

The Life of the Mind in a Field of Hay

There, across the pasture
laid flat beneath the sun,

long hour after hour, dry
round after round away,

tucked between the roots
of a sweetgum, within

a round shadow circumscribed
by the brightest light,

a quart jar of ice water,
the cool click and tumble

of leaves overhead. Soon,
soon I will be there.

To Let Go

I am tired of training.
MUHAMMED ALI

At the Agricultural Experiment Station
the boys are all over me the morning after:
no one missed the licking you took.
Their fists are up; they bob, weave, dance
forward and back. Each face is happy
under its hat. I pay off my bets,

thinking of Gary Scheiss, who waited tables
on his knees the last time you got beat.
I want to eat all the apple cobbler
and drink all the sweet cream. Who
has not dreamed to let go? So I grin
back as the boys count you out again.
You, still asleep this morning, the tip
of your tongue wetting your bruised lips.

With Ashes

There was a fire.
It took everything.
And still burns.

Each night flames hunt
through dead winter grass—

moonlight fills
a burnt field,
hangs like smoke

as the fires scatter.
Red eyes are everywhere outside.

In a thicket
flames lift like a choir.
You hear the music

when they move, taking a dark barn,
a shed, a house. Yours or mine.

The moon follows
and it is clear
what we've lost—

there is no telling where
the black earth ends, night begins.

Ask me who set the fire.

Muralist

For so many days and how slowly
he circles the concrete silo,
roof blown to the field he walks.
Each day a new detail, another
perspective. Figure and ground
always in his eyes, he moves off
to circle back in. In the distance
trees revolve, rising and falling.
Closer he counts the iron rungs
climbing its side to empty sky
and sees faces lightning has scored
into the concrete, blank, turned
forever toward moonlight and sun.
He steps inside the hollow dark
spinning looking up and out.

One more view from afar and now
he is ready. His eye, his hand.
He will match blues, browns, green
shades of the trees and fields.
He will paint away the gray concrete
edges that break the curves
of the earth. When the sky holds
only its sun and clouds pass by
unobstructed he will walk away,
leaving a roof, stunned birds,
a shadow no one can account for.

A Day in My Union Suit

Here, at last, is the fever
at sunrise, chills, the head
I can't lift from the pillow.
Each breath burns from
within, the quilts around me
become the whole world.
When I realize I won't die,
I can almost smile: nothing
could make me move.
The windows fill with cold
light, cattle in the fields
are rising. I see myself
loading hay into the truck,
riding over the hard ground,
counting new calves, hoping
that I won't find trouble.
I smile: right now, as
I breathe and let my eyes
close, there is probably trouble.

Celestial

To end this day
I shoot the black calf,
down so long
she would never rise,
so weak there is no
last shiver but mine.

In the ring of pines
off the highway I leave her,
poor hide and bones,
almost breathing.
Rank sacks of garbage
and yellow smoke roll
before a wind too sharp
for the flawless sky.

To end this day I wait
for a sign to release me.
In the waste I stand watch
with the spectacular sun,
the small, bone-white moon.
As if expecting words
I do not have, they lie
low on either horizon, each
round as the calf's round eye.

Mississippi

for my father

It is behind me now, that world
where nothing goes long without
breaking down, where the word
at the White Sand Grocery is
failure. A haybaler's shot, a fence
has washed away, Bobby Ladner's
moved out on his wife and kid.

Neither you nor I could stand it.
We each had to make the imperfect
world over: you were in my way,
I was in yours, no good came of it.
Anger, shouting, words worse
than blows in a blazing hayfield.
We couldn't just get by, like
the girl, who goes home to her family,
who expected as much. Bobby never
would settle down: bars in Louisiana,
women, he just wants everything
to come easy. Not in Mississippi,
where every tractor breaking bottomland
is close to collapse and you must

scratch by. Everybody's got his can
of old bolts, a bit of wire that'll do.
At the grocery you hear stories
of repairs in the field, home-made
remedies, the Chevy truck rebuilt
piece by piece. On the highway
I watched for them, their blue smoke,
their patchwork hoods in the mirror.
Just before the state line—Mississippi

welcome sign hanging awry—I passed
the last one. Somehow, in the cab
it was your face I saw, no longer
streaked with hay dust and tears.
It was you, waving your hand to me.

Horseshoes. Marfa, Texas.

Connect, connect. It's a refrain
I don't call out
or question. What and who
would I ask? The two old men
in straw hats and overalls
who walk from stake to stake
without a word to each other?
I watch summer dusk lift
the pecan trees of Marfa,
barren this year, into relief,
into the sky a blue
I'll call Mediterranean.
I lean against a trunk, suddenly
some Roman soldier under the leathery
lance-shaped leaves of an olive.
Wind off the sea rattling
through the leaves and my hair,
I never look up. I start pitching
my mule's lost shoe over
and over at a sharp white rock
as I wait for the afternoon
to blow away. It does.
Wind and the light move
over land and water, touching
who knows who. I don't. Marfa
is nowhere and what I have
are these two, absorbed
with the swing of their arms
and the flight of the shoe end

over end or in a slow flat spin.
Light gone, their eyes pinched
like mine in the dark
of these towering, still pecans,
I know they listen, hoping
for the familiar quick ring
of iron on iron
as their shoe strikes the stake
and they see the brief
true spark fly.

Lupe Dice Bueno

Lupe sleeps, his old belly full
of beer and sopapillas,
coffee-can pisspot by his bed,
the bunkhouse dark and quiet.
On our hands and knees
beyond his bed we hide
with the twelve dry rattles.
This evening near the barn
we saw him strike with the hoe
and the rattlesnake die belly-up.
No good he said, no rain.

He stirs in his sleep and we
stiffen. *Bueno* we hear him say.
He dreams of beer and sopapillas.
Or of rain, a slow summer night
rain over the whole prairie, ticking
his tin roof as he drinks his beer,
deep-fries the dough. Already
he sees the short grass freshen.
It will green by morning, sweet,
and the draws will run water.
Fence down at the water gaps,
the tanks in every pasture full.

Bueno he says in his sleep.
We think of women or horsepower.
We think of air-conditioned bars
in town and the music drumming.
This bunkhouse stinks of piss
and sweat. We work too hard,
girls in Rankin say our hands

are rough. We will see what they say
when we show them the rattles,
tell how fast old Lupe woke.
Bueno. It is not our vast dark
dry land tasting rain.

Those Who Stay On

Big Bend

Hot. More than one summer
will settle those who stay on
in Alpine or Marathon, miles
back from the border. A river.
It is the present tense, first
we must cross the desert.
There is no air, here we breathe
light, same as mesquite or cactus.
They live long, slow lives
storing light. Each one strikes
a pose: lean, held forever.

Boquillas

A boy is watching our burros.
Sun pins their shadows onto the dust.
Same dust, same canebrakes either
riverbank. What has changed?
I see an old man, trying to remember
the heat, the shade of this cantina,
long-neck bottles of Mexican beer.
I look ahead to look back. Will I
pause at the water's edge? What detail
will escape me? The time it took
to ride back, down the long hill?

Photograph. Mid-river.

Center-lens, the man with skiff
and burros. Eyes sharp as thorns
from seventy, eighty summers.
A background of pink bluffs cut
by the Rio Grande. Perfect light.
He stood as if he didn't care
what long life that moment had.
As if his hands felt the current
that would wash away the edges
of his face, the river that would
blur its own work in the distance.

South of the Border

There was a doctor in Juárez
who could work wonders.
He had a drug, some extract
doctors in the States didn't.
So my grandfather, at eighty
the arthritis in his knees worse
every day, planned his trip.
My grandmother would go too,
stout black Doris would drive.
Among them was not
one whole sentence in Spanish.
How then would they ask
for the goat's nuts?

*

Certain disaster, yet we kept
our counsel. We knew he dreamed
of rising from his chair, walking
like the young man he was
no longer. His first grandson,
I offered to go. It made sense—
Doris knew her way around
a kitchen but Ciudad Juárez
was no kitchen. And I'd had years
of Spanish. First from Señor Lopez,
the Cuban refugee whose tales
of skindiving and Havana nightlife
I still remember. Next came
Señora Anglade, a sweet widow
from Puerto Rico who baked
rum cakes and other delights

that melted on our tongues.
Therefore I was prepared. And how
I loved his dream of a land
of magic, all of it green
as the jungles of Quintana Roo,
where parrots squawked and strutted
their iridescent beaks and wings.
When it passed, when he came to
his senses and resigned himself
to aspirin and his armchair,
I wanted to whisper in his ear
like a shaman: Mexico, Mexico.

*

A bad bandit, Pancho Villa.
A week before I left, my grandfather
sat recollecting newspaper stories
seventy years old: how half
El Paso watched from their rooftops
while across the river Villa
sacked Ciudad Juárez. At eleven
too young to do anything
but dream how he could
straighten crooked Old Mexico out,
my grandfather missed his chance.
I might have told him how Villa
the bandit learned to read in jail,
the print of *Don Quijote* a mystery
unfolding at the tip of his thick
broken fingernails, but I did not.
Sancho Panza ran off at the mouth,
I simply listened: *You watch out
for bandits* and *Don't forget
my present—bring me back a parrot.*

Five hours to kill
before my train into the heart
of Mexico. The sun's a red chile
igniting the air filled
with dust and diesel fumes
from trucks idling in inspection lines.
I learn patience, I learn
confusion, I learn the language
of bordertown beggars, jabber
of lies and curses nothing like
my high school Spanish. Rote
is worthless here. Where in the book
is *chingado*? As the station fills
with Mexicans bound for home,
I construct a little fortress
with my bags and try to keep
a sharp eye on everything.

*

How far the *campesinos* walk
each Sunday, to mass and to market,
driving their angelic burros
over the dusty rocky roads or bearing
their wares on their own backs.
Hundreds come, to sell and buy
and barter, to amble in the sunny
plaza Nuestra Señora de la Salud.
Amid all the slow locomotion
and fast talk even I recognize,
among the many faces I see one
which without doubt belongs
to the most ancient of all Mexican women.
Beneath her bright shawl her eyes

radiate lines in every direction
across her face, which she offers
to me without pleading. And what
in each veined hand does she carry
but an ornate bamboo cage in which sing
and dart birds of all shapes and sizes,
among them one red and yellow and green,
oh so green, parrot, *papagayo*.

*

Oh my grandfather, were there not
laws, not lines at the border, agents
intent on keeping the wonderful
from us. Or were I Pancho Villa,
ready to break all laws but my own,
a knife in my teeth as I ride
across the river and into Texas,
bearing on my shoulder the beautiful
green *papagayo* for mile after mile
to your side. Together we'd sit
and dream listening to endless bright
syllables of *Mexico, Mexico, Mexico*

New Shoes

Today I'm far from Howard Hughes,
rich and sick with suspicion,
shuffling through the spare rooms
of his Desert Inn suite
with Kleenex boxes on his feet.
How sad. Mandarin of fear,
fingernails long as those Tz'u-shi
held out against the world,
Howard died in flight

above this country. This morning
I joined the tourists and retirees
wandering the labyrinthine
market stalls, butchering Spanish
to ask *How much?*
for guavas, mangoes, coconuts.
Sores on her hands, a woman
snapped flies from gold and green
pyramids of fruit. *Veinte y cinco.*
The gringo price. I paid it
and she handed over one
great coconut, tough of hide,
filled inside with wonders. I drank
the milk down and sat myself
on the curb, shooing away dogs
and smearing the sweet pulp

all over my new sandals
handmade of leather and old tires.
I slipped my tender feet in
and felt alive, invulnerable
of spirit as I lost myself

in the twisting, crowded streets.
Safer than the rich Mr. Hughes
in his Lear jet, in my new shoes,
my *guaraches de coco*, I sailed over
shit and trash and broken glass
without a worry, greeting everyone
with a wave, a good word, *Salud*.

Alta Gente

Oil up your body, your *cuerpo*,
and bake like a brick
on the balcony. On the wall
in their terra-cotta pots
the flowers will watch over you,
red as lollipops. Close
your blue eyes, lay your book
aside. Over the wall, down
in the street children shouting
sharp, colorful phrases
will bust bottle after bottle
in your honor. Don't misunderstand
the little pebbles that come
whistling down, tossed up
in your honor from the street
into the sun, intense and high
above your body, *tu cuerpo blanco*.

Sleepless

The high savage song the mosquito
each night brings
to my ear is not song,
I know. It's his tiny wings
so many times per second somewhere
in the dark above our bed.
The clock-tick is not song,
nor is the fountain outside
with its fretful pooling
and falling water song.
The savage wings sweep close,
I swipe at the sound and you
shift beneath the covers, settle
into the unlabored breathing
that is your gift and not mine.
I turn toward you and away, rocking
myself fitfully. It didn't work
to stand at the window
and count the village lights,
trying to match them one by one
with the scatter of stars.
One or the other was forever going out.
Over and over. I turn toward you
and away minute by minute
and yet you do not wake. I think
my eyes have never been more open
as I lie under the black canopy
of our bed, looking for one star,
one star which is light
and not the siren, distant
but closing, of blood for blood.
I will not wake you. You sleep.

La Hondonada

We walk along the ravine
and your sons run ahead, darting
around mesquite with its long thorns,
loose shale slipping
under their feet, their open hands
reaching forward. You find
in them the eternal question
What's next? What's next?
I'd like to know and to know
how perilous the world is really.
Is it possible we aren't walking
toward the worst possible?
I suppose calamity could be nothing
but a pinpoint of flame
deep in the brain. To extinguish it
we open our skulls to the wind.
To no end: calamity's the trick
candle we can't blow out
for good, the old volcano smoking
its cigarette, just waiting.

Nathan. Arden. The cliff drops
straight down three hundred feet.
Your stomach's at the bottom already,
lifeless among boulders, muddy pools.
What is the last safe point?
Nate calls back his dog, romping
at the lip—*Quesi!*—and they return
to your side to touch you,
to hook a finger in your belt loop
and walk beside you. Their cheeks
flushed, they spin out stories

from schoolbooks of human sacrifice.
The Iroquois at Niagara,
Mayans who pitched virgins
into deep jungle pools. Bound
with snakes of silver, weighted
with necklaces and totems
of the dark, eternal gods, one
goes down through the green water.
We see the bubbles rising
around her, we see her open eyes,
her doomed, beautiful face
as the jade face of a jaguar
drifts up from her throat
to kiss her, kiss her as she sinks.

Esperanza

Far down Homobono,
the *barrio* street you walk
each morning, I see you Esperanza—
short, full-bosomed,
with that name—Hope—you've buried
beneath a gravity that is complete
and cruel and troubling.
Esperanza, what are you to me
that I spend hours wondering what
breech of custom, what in ignorance
I have done or said
to so sour you? Your black hair
a head above the gangs of children
swirling around you lost
in street games, soccer and keep-away,
you advance, resolute, choosing
a certain cobblestone for each step
up the steep hill. It seems you
do not hear or see those children
or the beggars' tin cups full of sunlight
or the dogs nosing through garbage,
growling from alleys as you pass.
You have nothing for them this morning
or any other, only the dignity
of a maid to the rich. Your breath
grows short and fast but you won't stop
and you won't stop your whispering.
You whisper to yourself the whole way,
some prayer or string of curses
I've yet to hear and I've listened.
In my house you cook and clean all day
in a silence absolute to the ear

I put to my study door, a silence
I've tried to break with my own
or with questions it's your duty
to answer. You have a husband,
two sons, nine children in all.
The *carnitas* are best on Insurgentes.
You can think of no fiesta coming.
The word for squash, *calabaza*.
Shot-glass is *copita*. You give me
the words for loss and dream and wonder
before you go back to your broom
and I go back behind my door
with my *copita* and my longing.
The forms of verbs, Esperanza—
present, past and future indicative,
the imperfect and imperative,
reflexive, passive, radical
changing verbs—all are beyond me.
I'm unable to put into motion
the most elementary noun: the wind
that scatters the trash or blows
from town to bring me bells
or a burro, rooster, radio, anything
but this silence. *Yo espero,*
I hope, I wait. Esperanza,
criada of distance and whispers,
will you never enter this room
unbidden to disturb me and answer
what it is I do not ask: how long
must I wait and is there hope
you will smile and speak and bless me?

Other Titles in the Contemporary Poetry Series